ONE GOOD MARRIAGE

(that one, that one)

ONE GOOD MARRIAGE

SEAN REYCRAFT

One Good Marriage (that one, that one)
first published 2004 by
Scirocco Drama
An imprint of J. Gordon Shillingford Publishing Inc.

Scirocco Drama Editor: Glenda MacFarlane
Cover image by Field Day Inc.
Cover photo by Marina Dempster
Cover design by Terry Gallagher/Doowah Design Inc.
Author photo by Dan Cremin
Printed and bound in Canada

We acknowledge the financial support of The Canada Council for the Arts and the Manitoba Arts Council for our publishing program.

Canadian Cataloguing in Publication Data

Reycraft, Sean
One good marriage/Sean Reycraft.
A play.
ISBN 0-920486-57-6
I. Title.
PS8635.E92O54 2004 C812'.6 C2004-901542-7

J. Gordon Shillingford Publishing
P.O. Box 86, RPO Corydon Avenue, Winnipeg, MB Canada R3M 3S3

for my parents

Sean Reycraft

Born in Glencoe, Ontario, Sean Reycraft's plays include *Roundabout, The End of Dancing, Throat, Reconstruction* and *Einstein and the Relativity of Dreams*. His play *Pop Song* won the 2001 Chalmers Canadian Play Award and was published in *Shakin' the Stage: Four Plays from Theatre Direct Canada's Buncha Young Artists...Festival* (Scirocco Drama, 2003). He is graduate of Ryerson Theatre School and the Canadian Film Centre and currently lives in Toronto.

Production History

One Good Marriage (that one, that one) premiered at Theatre Passe Muraille, Toronto, in January 2004, with the following cast and crew:

STEWART .... Jeff Miller
STEPH .... Mary Francis Moore

Directed by Shari Hollett
Set and Lighting Design by Steve Lucas
Musical Composition by J.D. Nicholsen
Stage Manager: Monica Esteves

An earlier version of the play appeared as part of the 2002 SummerWorks Festival, and the playwright wishes to thank Franco Boni and Ruth Madoc-Jones for their involvement. Thanks also to Layne Coleman, The Regent Theatre (Picton), Stephen Finney, Randa Douche, Mickey Wagg and Brendan Wall.

On a near-empty stage, two chairs face the audience. Above is a banner reading, "Happy Anniversary"—only part hangs down, so all is seen is "versary". An upbeat love song plays.

STEWART enters from backstage. He is conservatively dressed. He looks around, eyeing the exits. Seeing nothing, he waits. After a few moments, STEPH appears. She walks to him, they look to each other for strength.

STEWART smiles at the audience, but before he can say anything—

STEPH: Everybody died.

STEWART's irritated.

STEPH: Everybody's dead.

STEWART smiles at the audience.

STEPH: But thanks for coming.

STEWART: See, I wouldn't start—

STEPH: Thanks for being here.

STEWART: Not like that.

STEPH: Thanks for showing up.

STEWART: I'd work the room, you know?

STEPH: You look good.

STEWART: I'd take my time.

STEPH: You look really good.

STEWART: I'd toss back a couple.

STEPH: You look great.

STEWART: I'd say some hellos.

STEPH: Hel-lo.

STEWART: And then—maybe then.

STEPH: Everybody died.

STEWART groans in misery.

Everybody's dead.

STEWART smiles at the audience.

It's too bad there's no pictures.

STEWART: See, I'd be less "out with it".

STEPH: I could show you pictures.

STEWART: I'd skate around the subject.

STEPH: It's too bad there's no video.

STEWART: I'd try some subtlety.

STEPH: I'd pop in the video.

STEWART: I'd start by talking about, say, you.

STEPH: I'd like to have something to show people.

STEWART: Let's talk about you.

STEPH: I only got stories.

STEWART: *(Aside to STEPH.)* Have stories.

STEPH: I only got them.

STEWART: And then—only then—

STEPH: But thanks for coming.

STEWART: That's when I'd start.

STEWART claps his hands together, then motions to the audience.

So about you—?

STEPH: Stewart?

STEWART: What?

STEPH: Stewart?

STEWART: Yeah?

STEPH: Stu?

STEWART: *(Tenderly.)* Close your eyes. Steph?

She closes her eyes. Blackout. A dim pool of light illuminates STEPH. Quietly—

Think of a pencil—a blue pencil, one of the "pencil crayon" kinds.

Beat.

Think of a mop—a gray string mop—all yellow from cleaning up mustard.

Beat.

Think of a Christmas tree stand—not the tree skirt, just the green steel stand.

Beat.

Steph?

Lights up. STEPH opens her eyes. Building in momentum—

STEPH: We met.

STEWART: We did.

STEPH: Him and me.

STEWART: It was a meeting—an actual meeting.

STEPH: There were tables organized.

STEWART: Chairs lined up.

STEPH: An agreed start time.

STEWART: An estimated finish.

STEPH: A topic for discussion.

STEWART: And teenagers.

STEPH: There were teenagers.

STEWART: Not many, maybe seven. But teenagers were there.

STEPH: Glencoe District.

STEWART: It's a high school.

STEPH: He runs the book club.

STEWART: I do. *(Proudly.)* I run an after-school book club.

STEPH: I sat in.

STEWART: She'd just started.

STEPH: I wanted to sit in.

STEWART: She'd transferred.

STEPH: He let me sit in.

STEWART: I can do that. *(Again—proudly.)* I'm the staff advisor.

STEPH: That's his title.

STEWART: It's more like "staff supervisor". To be an actual "staff advisor", you'd have to actually dispense staff-worthy advice. And to dispense staff-worthy advice you'd have to actually read the book.

STEPH: He's the librarian.

STEWART: Glencoe District High School's high school librarian.

STEPH: He never reads the book.

STEWART: I'm more of an "order and file" kinda guy.

STEPH: But it justifies your job.

STEWART: It does.

STEPH: "Staff Advisor for Glencoe District High School's Book Club".

STEWART: It justifies my job.

STEPH: I taught English.

STEWART: Like the language.

STEPH: And drama—I sometimes taught that.

STEWART: But you have to understand—this? *(Gesturing to STEPH.)* This here? It's not a "book" thing.

STEPH: It's not.

STEWART: It's not a "let's share reading" thing.

STEPH: It's really not.

STEWART: It's not a "you sit there with your book while I sit here with mine and I'll talk to you in four hours" kinda love.

STEPH: It's deeper.

STEWART: It was. It is.

STEPH: We just met at a book club.

STEWART: A high school book club.

STEPH: A really dull book club.

STEWART: It helps if you read the book.

STEPH: He stared.

STEWART looks at STEPH.

STEWART: I just stared.

STEPH looks at STEWART.

STEPH: And I stared—I stared back.

Brief pause.

STEWART: A few months went by—

STEPH: I'm thirsty.

STEWART: We dated awhile.

STEPH: I'm getting thirsty.

STEWART: She'd had this apartment.

STEPH: My throat's got a scratch.

STEWART: On Fridays I'd drive over.

STEPH: I'm parched.

STEWART: We'd sail into London for a movie.

STEPH: I'm very parched.

STEWART: We'd see a movie.

STEPH: This is parched.

STEWART: We'd go for snacks and a pint.

STEPH: I'd like a pint.

STEWART: I took her around—she met my parents. They talked about foreign oppression and 70s TV shows. *(Beat.)* Not foreign oppression *in* 70s TV shows. They talked about foreign oppression. Then they talked about 70s TV shows—the kind everybody used to watch.

STEPH: Stewart?

STEWART: I met her mother. Nice woman.

STEPH: Stewart.

STEWART: A little lonely with a little too much perfume, but she was okay.

STEPH: Get me water.

STEPH realizes he's not listening to her. Almost begrudgingly, she picks up the story.

It's all right.

STEWART: At school we were big gossip.

STEPH: It's okay.

STEWART: An "it" couple.

STEPH: I'm not thirsty.

STEWART: I've never been part of an "it" couple.

STEPH: Not no more.

STEWART: *(Aside to STEPH.)* Any.

STEPH: Not any more.

STEWART: We got whispered about in hallways.

STEPH: I got smooching sounds in the class.

STEWART: I got love notes in returned books.

STEPH: They made sexual gestures behind my back.

STEWART: In the bathrooms—I found diagrams.

STEPH: *(Aside to STEWART.)* You mean graffiti.

STEWART: I mean diagrams.

STEPH: Of you—me?

STEWART: If they were graffiti, I'd say they were graffiti.

STEPH: You never told me.

STEWART: It would've upset you.

STEPH: You never told me.

STEWART: You would have got mad.

STEPH: You should have told me.

STEWART: *(Explaining for the audience.)* It was a "this is how Mister puts his thing in Miss" kinda scribble.

STEPH: I'm not mad.

STEWART: Some student with too much time.

STEPH: An art student.

STEWART: An art student with too little creativity and too much time.

STEPH: I hate art.

STEWART: More than reading.

Brief pause.

STEPH: I'm cold

STEWART: So we met.

STEPH: You getting cold?

STEWART: So we dated.

STEPH: I'm freezing.

STEWART: It's the middle of summer.

STEPH: I'm still cold.

STEWART: So we met.

STEPH: I am.

STEWART: So we dated.

STEPH: I had a little "thing" with my ex-boyfriend, but he knows about that—Stewart does. We've talked about that.

STEWART: She slipped and I ignored it.

STEPH: I slipped.

STEWART: And I ignored it. After that we were good. After that we were great.

STEPH: Then he asked me.

STEWART: At Christmas. It's a special time, Christmas.

STEPH: It was sentimental but not cutesy.

STEWART: She doesn't like cutesy.

STEPH: I don't like it.

STEWART: She's very hard.

STEPH: I fuckin' hate it.

STEWART: She's fucking kidding.

STEPH: I fucking am. I got pictures—

STEWART: *(Aside to STEPH.)* Have—

STEPH: *Have* pictures—velvet pictures—of unicorns, puppy dogs and big swooping rainbows saved up from when I was a girl. As a teenager I considered Disney characters suitable role models. I wore my grandma's charm bracelet up until a few months ago and Wednesdays at nine, I cry—I always cry at the end of *West Wing*.

STEWART: So we met.

STEPH: Him and me.

STEWART: So we dated.

STEPH: We dated some more.

STEWART: And then I asked her.

STEPH: He proposed.

STEWART: She said, "yes".

STEPH: I said, "okay".

STEWART: She said, "okay" and we got married.

STEPH: That summer.

STEWART: That August.

STEPH: We planned this carefully.

STEWART: Strategized this out.

STEPH: Not July—we needed time.

STEWART: We did—sufficient time. And not June—

STEPH: We still had school.

STEWART: We picked a month.

STEPH: We chose a day.

STEWART: We hired a minister.

STEPH: We booked his church.

STEWART: Invites got printed.

STEPH: Invites went out.

STEWART: A tux was rented.

STEPH: A dress got bought.

STEWART: A dress got mortgaged.

STEPH: It was off-white and trailing.

STEWART: And food.

STEPH: A selection of salads.

STEWART: Potato salad.

STEPH: Caesar salad.

STEWART: Maybe—yeah, maybe even coleslaw.

STEPH: We wanted ample vegetarian alternatives.

STEWART: And then we wanted meat.

STEPH: Lots of meat.

STEWART: We wanted beef.

STEPH: Roast beef to feed our guests.

STEWART: Yes, but who to toss the salads—who to cook the beef?

STEPH: The Ladies' Legion Auxiliary.

STEWART: The Glencoe Ladies' Legion Auxiliary.

STEPH: We saved money. They were pretty cheap.

STEWART: Now the hall—

STEPH's mood darkens.

STEPH: Right. The hall.

STEWART: You okay?

STEPH: I'm good.

STEWART: You all right?

STEPH: I'm still a little cold.

STEWART leans forward.

STEWART: Sheila Walker—she's a girl in town.

STEPH: Nice girl.

STEWART: I'd say she's— "pretty".

STEPH: She's—what? Twenty-two? Twenty-three?

STEWART: Sheila Walker's father owns the IGA.

STEPH: Sheila Walker's husband—he's a dentist.

STEWART: Sheila Walker's goal in life is to have children—maybe two, maybe six—to rule the world and all the money in it.

STEPH: Sheila Walker thinks that big.

STEWART: She does—and because Sheila Walker thinks that big, Sheila Walker needs to be organized. And because Sheila Walker's organized, she booked the Glencoe Community Centre twenty-six months in advance.

STEPH: I hate Sheila Walker.

STEWART: *(Almost overlapping.)* We hate Sheila Walker.

STEPH: And her children—I'll really hate them.

Beat.

STEWART: That left us with the Legion.

STEPH: The Glencoe Branch of the Royal Canadian Legion.

STEWART: And the gym.

STEPH: *(Correcting STEWART.)* It never left us with the gym.

STEWART: We could have had it in the gym.

STEPH: You don't have gym weddings.

STEWART: You do.

STEPH: They're called "proms".

Brief pause. STEPH looks around anxiously.

STEPH: You hungry?

STEWART: It was a small town.

STEPH: I'm getting hungry.

STEWART: It was a small church.

STEPH: I'm kinda peck-ish.

STEWART: We had a small wedding.

STEPH smiles to the audience.

STEPH: It made big sense.

STEWART: And everybody came.

STEPH: Everybody showed.

STEWART: Parents. Her grandparents. Some brothers. Sisters. And that's just family. Add in a university buddy, some folks from the staff room and the girl who cuts our hair—

STEPH: The band.

STEWART: The 70s tribute band—and soon you're serving eighty-six. *(STEWART becomes fidgety.)* But we're not gonna talk about that.

STEPH: Maybe a little.

STEWART: We shouldn't talk about that.

STEPH: Maybe a bit. *(STEPH stands, moving away from STEWART.)* I had nerves.

STEWART: *(STEWART laughs at the memory.)* She had nerves.

STEPH: I threw up outside. And his college roommate—?

STEWART: *(STEWART stands, panicked.)* Don't.

STEPH: The "best man"?

STEWART: Don't tell them that.

STEPH: "You could do posters."

STEWART: He didn't say it as an insult.

STEPH: "Be naked on posters."

STEWART: It's not *exactly* an insult.

STEPH: "I'd buy that poster."

STEWART: *(Turning to the audience.)* It's something to say.

STEPH: We won't talk about the wedding.

STEWART: All right.

STEPH: We won't talk about leaving, waving—saying "goodbye".

STEWART: Okay.

STEPH: We won't talk about any of that.

STEWART notices as STEPH's overwhelmed with emotion.

STEWART: Steph?

STEPH: 'Cause it's not about that.

STEWART: Steph.

STEPH: It's about what happened after—and all that happened after.

STEWART: Steph?

STEPH: Yeah?

STEWART: *(Tenderly.)* Close your eyes.

STEPH: For a minute.

STEWART: Close 'em, okay?

STEPH: For just a minute.

Blackout. STEPH's illuminated in a dim pool of light. Quietly—

STEWART: Think of a blue lampshade. Not a big lampshade—more like the kind you'd find on a table lamp.

Beat.

Think of a soap dispenser—the kind you find at a movie theatre with the pink stuff showing through.

Beat.

Think of a TV remote—not a big complicated one, just the numbers with a button for "on" and "off".

Beat.

And?

Lights up. STEPH opens her eyes. Building in momentum—

STEPH: We met.

STEWART: We did.

STEPH: We got married.

STEWART: We did.

STEPH: We had a honeymoon.

STEWART: A simple honeymoon.

STEPH: Nothing flashy—no need for extravagance.

STEWART: "Focus on the romance".

STEPH: *(A little embarrassed.)* I said that—I did.

STEWART: She's a teacher—I'm a librarian.

STEPH: We can't afford Italy. We can't afford Hawaii.

STEWART: Las Vegas?

STEPH: The Virgin Islands?

STEWART: We can't even afford Niagara Falls.

STEPH: *(Aside to STEWART.)* Well, we can.

STEWART: I'm talking spiritually.

STEPH: I said, "Find me a shack—a little shack. Something like it's out of a horror movie. Or a spy movie. Or that movie with Sissy Spacek where everybody's really, really poor. Find me something secluded. Find me something private. Find me someplace nobody would ever think to live in and that—that is where you and I will celebrate the blessed union of our love."

STEWART: It sounded interesting.

STEPH sits.

STEPH: It sounded stupid.

STEWART: It sounded intriguing.

STEWART: It sounded dumb, but it sounded like things sound when you're getting married. When you're planning a honeymoon. When you're in love.

STEWART sits.

STEWART: We drove six hours.

STEPH: I stayed awake for two.

STEWART: *(Aside to STEPH.)* You stayed awake for twenty minutes.

STEPH: My eyes got tired with the driving.

STEWART: Your eyes got tired with the drinking.

STEPH: First night we stayed at a motel.

STEWART: The "Motel 6" in Pembroke. In the morning we kept driving north.

STEPH: *(Interrupting.)* I wanna say something.

STEWART: Steph—

STEPH: I have to say something. *(Beat.)* I wanted to check.

STEWART: Steph—

STEPH: Call home—I wanted to do that. But I didn't. And I don't feel bad I didn't. I don't feel good I didn't, either. I don't feel anything, really—it's just something to mention.

Brief pause.

STEWART: So the shack.

STEPH: The shack.

STEWART: The shack wasn't a shack.

STEPH: The shack was shit.

STEWART moves downstage to the audience.

STEWART: A farmer near Chalk River—he'd rented it to me. I'd met him in a coffee shop when he saw me eyeing the "cottage for rent" signs. He said he used it for huntin' in winter. He said it was spacious but simple. He said it had served him well for over forty years. This farmer? This farmer had four teeth and a wandering eye. And when I saw it? When I saw his simple but spacious shack? All I could think was, "many, many dead things have been dragged back here".

STEPH: That's not what you want to be thinking the day after our nuptials.

STEWART: *(To STEPH.)* Our what?

STEPH: Our nuptials.

STEWART falls back into his seat.

STEWART: I wanna be thinking about sex.

STEPH: Hot sex.

STEWART: You wanna be thinking about that.

STEPH: Still, we didn't go—not right away.

STEWART: You didn't want to.

STEPH: I didn't. I got determined.

STEWART: You got insistent.

STEPH: I got proactive. I thought, "Let's use our honeymoon to really get to know each other."

STEWART: We stayed two weeks at the "Motel 6".

STEPH: The pool was busted.

STEWART: The air conditioning wasn't.

STEPH: We got to know each other.

STEWART: We got to know each other all right.

STEPH: And then—

STEWART: Then.

STEPH: Then we headed home.

STEWART: Six hours.

STEPH: We headed home.

Beat. STEWART can't continue with the story—not yet. STEWART looks at STEPH—

STEWART: You thirsty? You cold? You hot?

She isn't.

You have a headache? Tired? Achy? Itchy? Nervous? You—

STEPH: I'm good.

STEWART: Steph?

STEPH: I'm fine.

STEWART turns back to the audience.

STEWART: To get back to my house—

STEPH: Our house.

Beat.

STEWART: To get to what was "my" house but is now "our" house you have to turn off the County Road and head down Main Street—Main Street being the main street through Glencoe.

STEPH: So we did that.

STEWART: We turned—we drove down Main Street.

STEPH: I told him we should stop at the Becker's.

STEWART: I heard and had no problem with that suggestion. So we did—we stopped at the Becker's.

STEPH: I bought some milk, some bread.

STEWART: And pop.

STEPH: I wanted pop. And cigarettes—you bought some of them.

STEWART: I do that when I feel edgy.

STEPH: He often feels "edgy".

STEWART: I often buy cigarettes.

STEPH: The first "sign"? The first "indication" things weren't swell?

STEWART: Mrs. Pazitka behind the counter didn't ask about the honeymoon.

STEPH: Not that she was required.

STEWART: It's not like it's her job.

STEPH: That's to run the Becker's.

STEWART: Still—it is a courtesy.

STEPH: And we'd have answered if she did. We'd have told her about the shack and the motel with the busted swimming pool and we'd all have a laugh—a great big laugh. An "ain't life funny" kinda laugh.

STEWART: But she didn't ask anything. Not even, "Is that gonna be all?"

STEPH: She just smiled like the Becker's was vacuuming her empty and gave me my change. She shorted me a nickel—I know 'cause I counted.

STEWART: The rest of Main Street—

STEPH: We're not just talking road.

STEWART: Sidewalks. Stores. Even lights in houses.

STEPH: No sign of anything.

STEWART: No sign of life.

STEPH: We turned down our street.

STEWART: What was "my" street and now officially is "ours".

STEPH: We pulled into the driveway.

STEWART: Our driveway to our home.

STEPH: He popped the trunk.

STEWART: Our trunk. I opened the car door and grabbed a few things.

STEPH: I followed—along the driveway and up the porch steps.

STEWART: Our porch. Our steps.

Brief pause. STEWART stands, moving downstage and away from STEPH.

There were cards.

STEPH: A porch of cards.

STEWART: There were flowers and pictures and flowers and cards.

STEPH: The door—you couldn't open it.

STEWART: It got stuck—it got stuck tight with cards.

STEPH: I tried to open it—

STEWART: But the cards—

STEPH: I pushed.

STEWART: They jammed—they got stuck.

STEPH: I shoved 'em back hard.

STEWART: She was vicious.

STEPH: I was aggressive. You spend two weeks at the "Motel 6" in Pembroke, you're not getting locked out by a bunch of cards.

Brief pause.

STEWART: Out of the corner of my eye.

STEPH: I didn't see it.

STEWART: This eye—this right corner here.

STEPH: I was down the hallway.

STEWART: I see this shape walking with purpose.

STEPH: About halfway down the hallway.

STEWART: I see this figure walking with direction.

STEPH: Then I was out of the hallway and into the kitchen.

STEWART: Walking like it's walked this walk to our place a thousand times before—but it hadn't. It'd never walked this walk to our place before. She had never been over. She had never even said, "nice day".

STEWART pulls out a pack of cigarettes, placing one in his mouth.

STEWART: I think she was afraid of me—afraid of the single librarian living alone. "Now that I'm married"—that's what I thought—"Now that I'm married's when she wants to say hello."

STEWART lights the cigarette in his mouth.

STEWART: My neighbour—

STEPH: *Our* neighbour.

STEWART: "Trish".

STEPH: Early '40s.

STEWART: Blonde hair.

STEPH: Kinda scary in an "anorexic with a Honda" kinda way.

STEWART: Trish was divorced with a second husband and two children—

STEPH: Two male children—

STEWART: Twin male children from her first marriage.

STEPH: Twin male children I was going to be teaching that year. Twin male children I was dreading teaching that year.

STEWART: Her actual name? Her actual name was "Trish-a".

STEPH: "Trish" was her "call me" name.

STEWART: As in "call me Trish".

STEPH: And we did. We called her Trish.

STEWART: So here she was walking with purpose.

STEPH stands, moving downstage and away from STEWART.

STEPH: I told you—I didn't see her.

STEWART: Here she came walking with direction.

STEPH: I was in the kitchen.

STEWART: Here she was walking like she'd walked the walk a thousand times before.

STEPH: The phone was blinking.

STEWART: She hadn't walked the walk a thousand times before.

STEPH: There's "messages" when it's blinking.

STEWART: But with Steph and me being absent—

STEPH: The phone in the kitchen was blinking.

STEWART: With me and Steph being away—

STEPH: We had messages.

STEWART: And Trish had something to tell us.

Brief pause. Both stand at opposite ends of the stage.

STEPH: We got the news separately.

STEWART: Trish sat me down.

STEPH: I hollered I was on the phone.

STEWART: Trish asked if I wanted water. Maybe pop. Maybe beer. Then she offered tea.

STEPH: His mailbox—

STEWART: Who drinks "tea"?

STEPH: Our mailbox was full.

STEWART: Trish started to cry.

STEPH: Every message the same thing.

STEWART: Then she really started to cry.

STEPH: Over and over, the same thing.

STEWART: Her shoulders started shaking.

STEPH: Skip to the next message.

STEWART: Her shoulders stopped shaking.

STEPH: Skip to the next message.

STEWART: Trish stopped crying.

STEPH: Skip all the way to the end.

STEWART: Trish's whole "venting of deeply felt emotion" —?

STEPH: I got to the end.

STEWART: Everything stopped as Trish waited for Steph.

STEPH: I put the phone down.

STEWART: Trish got tired of waiting for you.

STEPH: I put the phone down.

STEWART: Not bored—just tired.

STEPH: I put the phone down.

Long pause as STEWART puts his cigarette out, and then returns downstage.

STEWART: Oh, she was good about it—she was like a pro. She stuck with the "I'm sorry's" while never moving into the "I know what you're going through's". Since then I've heard worse. Since then I've heard, "Death is but a shadow 'cross the pathway of heaven". I've heard, "Tomorrow is a mystery not answered today". And I've heard, "What the caterpillar thinks is an ending, the butterfly knows is a beginning". But not Trish. She didn't say any of that. Just a whole lot of "I'm sorrys" and "I'm so sorrys". Okay, and maybe one, "I can't imagine how you feel".

Brief pause.

I did the requisite, "No—"

STEPH: "That's not possible."

STEWART: "Can you say that again?"

STEPH: "And again?"

STEWART: "And again."

STEPH: "Okay, thanks."

STEWART: "No—I'm sorry, one more time—?"

Long pause. STEWART turns away, collapsing into his chair. STEPH remains standing at the far corner of the stage.

STEWART: After Trish left I had that beer.

STEPH: I didn't want beer. I was in the mood for tea.

STEWART: I opened the fridge door. I pulled out the bottle.

STEPH: I filled the kettle. I turned on the stove.

STEWART: I got the opener. I popped the top.

STEPH: I watched the gas. I waited for the whistle.

STEWART: I opened the fridge door. I got another beer.

STEPH: I lost interest in waiting. I turned off the stove.

STEWART: I watched TV.

STEPH: I watched the wall.

STEWART: I stayed downstairs.

STEPH: I went to bed.

STEWART: I followed her up.

STEPH: I closed my eyes—

Blackout. STEPH is illuminated in a dim pool of light—darker than any before. STEWART pushes himself out of his chair and moves behind her. STEPH starts to sob. STEWART calms her with—

STEWART: Think of a clothespin—but one of those wooden clothespins, not the cheap plastic kind.

Beat.

Think of a coffee cup—like a restaurant coffee cup with no design or anything just white.

Beat.

Think of a streetlight but how it looks in the day with the bulb part out.

Beat.

And?

Lights up. STEPH's calmed herself. STEWART stays standing behind.

STEPH: We met.

STEWART: We got married.

STEPH: There was a honeymoon.

STEWART: There was a motel.

STEPH: And then—we came home.

Brief pause. STEWART and STEPH both look out into the audience.

STEWART: Not everybody died.

STEPH: They didn't—not right away.

STEWART: My sister lived the night.

STEPH: My uncle made it to morning.

STEWART: The college roommate she was talking about—?

STEPH: "I'd-buy-your-poster" boy? The one I said—?

STEWART: Three days.

STEPH: They didn't think he'd make it.

STEWART: He didn't make it.

STEPH: They didn't think he'd make it so long.

STEWART: And Tessa.

STEPH: My Grandma.

STEWART: She had the best chance.

STEPH: She had no chance.

STEWART: She would've lived.

STEPH: She wasn't the "living kind".

STEWART: Twelve days it took to bury everybody.

STEPH breaks away from STEWART, moving across the stage.

STEPH: Eighty-six funerals.

STEWART: Eighty-six caskets.

STEPH: Eighty-six holes in the ground.

STEWART: Eighty-six prayers for the dead.

STEPH: And eighty-six headstones to mark them.

Brief pause.

STEWART: And us?

STEPH: And we?

STEWART: We must've been in Chalk River when the story hit—then back at the Motel 6 after that.

STEPH: We didn't know.

STEWART: We didn't listen to the radio—I'd made us some tapes.

STEPH: We didn't know.

STEWART: On TV we watched sitcoms. We never went near a paper. Reading was never on my mind.

STEPH: He's more of an "order and file" kinda guy.

STEWART: Before the wedding, we'd run into people on the street, in the supermarket—at parent/teacher night, anywhere we were. They'd ask about the honeymoon and look interested—they'd really want to know. They'd tell us not to worry. They'd advise us to get away—to really do that, really get away. And Steph and I—we took that advice.

STEPH: We didn't worry.

STEWART: We got away.

STEPH: We disappeared.

STEWART walks to STEPH.

STEWART: They tried to find us—they wanted to call—

STEPH: Everybody thought we were in a hunter's shack in the woods.

STEWART: So when we got back.

STEPH: When we drove back to town.

STEWART: All the funerals had been serviced. All the caskets had been closed. And that "good-bye" thing people do—?

STEPH: That "closure" part people need?

STEWART: We never got to do it.

STEPH: There was an almost.

STEWART: We don't talk—

STEPH: There was an almost that we almost attended.

STEWART: The minister—

STEPH: The one who'd married us—

STEWART: The one who blessed us.

STEPH: The one who said, "you're man and wife—now go".

STEWART: I didn't know there's a "hierarchy" thing. A "courtesy" thing. A whole "let the congregation go first" kinda deal. He was a minister—and because he was a minister, they decided to hold him back. Postpone the burial. I didn't know they did that. I didn't know.

STEPH: But we missed it.

STEWART: We stopped at a mall off the highway.

STEPH: We wanted to get some things for home.

STEWART: We wanted to get some souvenirs.

STEPH: So when we turned down Main Street.

STEWART: When she suggested we stop at the Becker's, everybody in town—

STEPH: They were at the cemetery.

STEWART: Everybody at the cemetery.

STEPH: Except—

STEWART: Except the exceptions.

STEPH: Mrs. Pazitka—she was working.

STEWART: *(Actually finding this funny.)* Mrs. Pazitka got left behind.

STEPH: And Trish.

STEWART: Trish. Trish was waiting.

STEWART breaks away from STEPH, escaping to the back of the stage.

STEPH: Stewart—?

STEWART's noticed the banner hanging down.

STEWART: The string.

STEPH: What?

STEWART: There's no string.

STEPH: What are you doing?

STEWART: On this end—where's the string?

Suddenly guilty, STEPH stares out and pretends that everything's okay.

STEPH: Talk about the shack again.

STEWART: You didn't finish stringing the banner?

STEPH: Tell that part—that part was good.

STEWART: You only tied half.

STEPH: I tied more than half.

STEWART: You didn't finish.

STEPH: I must'a stopped.

STEWART: Why'd you stop?

STEPH: *(Forcefully.)* I must'a just did.

STEWART collapses in a chair, his head in his hands. STEPH doesn't really know what to do. She smiles at the audience, then moves in behind STEWART. She places both hands on his back.

We met.

STEWART: We got married.

STEPH: There was a honeymoon.

STEWART: There was a motel.

STEPH: And then we came home.

STEWART: And.

STEPH: And.

STEWART looks up.

STEWART: And our "plan" —her and me—our little "plan".

STEPH: Our little purpose—

STEWART: Our little *reason* for having our wedding halfway through August.

STEPH: We wanted time—

STEWART: Not *a lot* of time—

STEPH: A little time before school started up.

STEWART: The time a new couple needs. Time for writing

"thank you" cards. For developing pictures, for pasting them in tasteful yet oversized albums to show off. And for hilarious yet romantic stories over things like chips and wine spritzers. But there was nobody to thank.

STEPH: No pictures to paste.

STEWART: And our stories—

STEPH: Our hilarious stories.

STEWART: Our romantic stories.

STEPH: There's another time to tell them.

STEWART: Instead, we called up relatives of late relatives—friends of late friends. People who'd known people who'd been at our wedding. We visited cemeteries. We wandered through graveyards. We held hands and said, "I'm sorry, I'm so sorry" like Trish did those few days back. And all those people who knew people who'd been at our wedding—

STEPH: And all those people who knew people—they wanted to be our friends.

STEWART: But their veil of blame—

STEPH: Their veil of blame.

STEWART: It's understandable.

STEPH: It's not hard to grasp.

STEWART: And our mountain of responsibility—our *Everest* of guilt. It's understandable.

STEPH: But so, so hard to grasp.

STEPH steps away from STEWART.

STEWART: And coming home—

STEPH: And coming back—

STEWART: And like before—

STEPH: Like oh so much before—

STEPH sits. Brief pause.

STEWART: Trish.

STEPH: "Not Trish-a, just call me Trish".

STEWART: She and some ladies had been "at it".

STEPH: Those were her words: "at it".

STEWART: And what she was "at" was in her freezer—

STEPH: Trish's deep freezer.

STEWART: For Trish is a woman who needs her freezer to be very, very deep.

STEPH: She had lasagna.

STEWART: She had shepherd's pie.

STEPH: She had chili.

STEWART: She had meat loaf.

STEPH: And squares.

STEWART: Chocolate squares.

STEPH: With bits of coconut.

STEWART: Who eats coconut?

STEPH: And butter tarts—just for us.

STEWART: And that's when I realized.

STEPH: That's when he knew.

STEWART: That's when I pulled you into the living room.

STEPH: You sat me down.

STEWART: *(Turning to STEPH.)* I sat across from you sorta like this—

STEPH: Sorta like now.

STEWART: —and that's when I looked at you and said, "Everybody died. Everybody's dead. And who we are left with? The only people we know?"

STEPH: Trish.

STEWART: Mr. Trish.

STEPH: Trish's twin male sons.

STEWART: Mrs. Pazitka.

STEPH: Sheila Walker.

STEWART: Sheila Walker's dentist husband.

STEPH: Sheila Walker's future children.

STEWART: And our high school principal. *(Beat.)* Which is funny, 'cause—

STEPH: Which is hysterical, 'cause—

STEWART: That's about when he called.

STEPH: He talked serious.

STEWART: He spoke using a solemn tone.

STEPH: He was offering condolences, sympathies.

STEWART: He offered us more time, but—

STEWART pushes himself out of his chair, moving downstage.

STEWART: —time for what? To adjust? To mourn? To remember? Why would I—

STEPH: Why would we.

STEWART: Why would we need that? What were the trips to the graveyards for? The planting of flowers? The driving for hours to visit people who did nothing but cry? Was he implying that I—

STEPH: That we.

STEWART: —that we hadn't somehow done all that? That we were cowards? That we were lazy? Or was he assuming that we were somehow unable to cope with the tragedy? "We don't need time," I told him—

STEPH: We.

STEWART: —we told him. We don't need time.

STEPH: I need the children.

STEWART: I need the book club.

STEPH: I need Trish's twin male sons.

STEWART: I need a paycheque.

STEPH: Two paycheques.

STEWART: We need a warning bell at a quarter to nine and another fifteen minutes later. We need periods and semesters and statutory holidays and maybe okay probably the occasional fire drill. We need lunch duty and assembly duty and an eagerness to catch smokers in the bathrooms. And we need comfort, that kind of comfort that teaching—or at least library-ing—for Glencoe District High School can bring.

STEPH: We said we'd be there.

STEWART: We said, "We appreciate your concern."

STEPH: We said, "We'll see ya".

STEWART: And that morning—that early September morning

we realized our time at Glencoe High was forever changed.

Long pause. STEWART sits beside STEPH. A slight smile crosses STEPH's face.

STEPH: It was better.

STEWART: It was *amazing.*

STEPH: No sexual gestures in assemblies.

STEWART: No diagrams in the stalls.

STEPH: No giggles from the back of the class.

STEWART: The library computers were no longer for surfing porn.

STEPH: Assignments were original works, not something copied.

STEWART: And nobody—not anybody asked me for books. Somehow, someway, they all looked everything up themselves.

STEPH: They read the readings—they wrote the writings.

STEWART: They let me pick the monthly book selection. I picked *Carrie* 'cause I'd seen the movie.

STEPH: Lunches.

STEWART: We never had to supervise.

STEPH: Dances.

STEWART: School dances, too.

STEPH: I hate to supervise.

STEWART: All that standing at the wall.

Beat.

STEPH: Even so.

STEWART: Even then it wasn't all "good" different.

STEPH: My language—my words—they started to go.

STEWART: Her tenses get mixed-up.

STEPH: My verb choice is bad.

STEWART: She's an English teacher.

STEPH: It's just bad. So—he corrects me.

STEWART: I correct her.

STEPH: It gets annoying.

STEWART: But I correct her.

STEPH: *(To STEWART.)* It gets annoying.

Brief pause.

STEWART: At the school the new teachers—

STEPH: The newly hired ones.

STEWART: The ones who replaced the teachers who died.

STEPH: They were freaked out.

STEWART: The old teachers—

STEPH: The ones we hadn't invited to our wedding.

STEWART: They seemed cautious.

STEPH: And the kids—

STEWART: They seemed edgy. Nervous.

STEPH: Try, "paranoid".

STEWART: They wanted to talk to us but they weren't sure how.

STEPH: We got asked our opinions on things like "sports teams".

STEWART: They'd ask, "Are you gonna watch the game"?

STEPH: They'd ask me "How do you think it's gonna turn out?"

STEWART: And food.

STEPH: The cafeteria food.

STEWART: They'd ask us, "What's good today?" and "What should I eat"?

STEPH: And the weather.

STEWART: Always the weather.

STEPH: "It's misty for a Monday."

STEWART: "Warm for a Wednesday".

STEPH: "It's getting colder, isn't it?"

STEWART: "How soon do you think it's gonna snow?"

STEPH: But never the summer.

STEWART: "How was your summer?"

STEPH: We never got asked that.

STEWART: We never did.

STEPH: *(Starting to lose it.)* 'Cause I'd tell them—I'd answer.

STEWART: Steph—?

STEPH: "You wanna know what my June, my July—my August was like?"

STEWART: Steph?

STEPH: What?

STEWART: Your—?

STEPH: Yeah.

STEWART: Close 'em for a minute, okay?

STEPH: Okay.

Blackout. A dim pool of light illuminates STEPH—only this time, she's restless, twitchy.

STEWART: Think of a towel—a white towel hanging on the back of a door to dry.

Brief pause. STEPH is trying to concentrate.

Think of a radiator painted brown—light brown 'cause it matches the room.

Brief pause. STEPH can't concentrate.

Think of an encyclopedia—but a really slim one like it's about everything that starts with "zed". Think of that on a bookshelf. Think of that collecting dust.

Brief pause. STEPH sighs. It's not working for her.

And?

Lights up. STEPH opens her eyes.

STEPH: We met.

STEWART: We got married.

STEPH: There was a honeymoon.

STEWART: There was a motel.

STEPH: We came home.

STEWART: And then—we had holidays. *(Quick to STEPH.)* You okay?

STEPH: I'm good.

STEWART: We've decided something.

STEPH: More like "realized" —but anyway.

STEWART: And maybe it was that time—that year.

STEPH: Maybe it was everything that happened.

STEWART: As a country, a people—? We have too many holidays.

STEPH: Too many "special" days.

STEWART: Too many days of celebration a year—and it's not "a lot" too many.

STEPH: As a teacher I normally wouldn't bring this up.

STEWART: And I don't know why we're whining.

STEPH: *(Aside to STEWART.)* We're not whining.

STEWART: I don't know why we're complaining.

STEPH: We're not complaining.

STEWART: I don't know why we're being emphatic.

STEPH: We're emphatic. We're that.

STEWART: Thanksgiving—we avoided.

STEPH: Not entirely.

STEWART: Not completely. We went to dinner.

STEPH: Swiss Chalet and a movie.

STEWART: We saw a movie.

STEPH: A Jennifer Lopez movie. She wore a wig. It made me cry.

STEWART: After, we ordered snacks and a pint.

STEPH: Our usual pint.

STEWART: Which became two.

STEPH: Which became four.

STEWART: Which became *nine. (Brief pause.)* Next holiday, we vowed, would be different.

STEPH: Everything was gonna change, but—

STEWART: Halloween! *(Beat.)* Nobody knocked.

STEPH: Nobody wanted our candy.

STEWART: We're teachers.

STEPH: We're a child's trusted destination.

STEWART: We bought chocolate bars.

STEPH: Whole ones—not the little kind. And cans of pop.

STEWART: Brand name.

STEPH: Not discount.

STEWART: They weren't apples.

STEPH: We weren't giving out apples.

STEWART: For years I would ignore the door.

STEPH: I'd leave my lights out.

STEWART: I'd hide in the basement.

STEPH: I'd leave my lights out.

STEWART: And here we were.

STEPH: Married.

STEWART: A couple.

STEPH: Anticipating the arrival of overweight greedy children.

STEWART: Hoping to say, "hey honey—look at this. He's an astronaut."

STEPH: "She's a fairy princess."

STEWART: "Ballerinas—all around!"

STEPH: But nothing.

STEWART: Nobody. And not just that—

STEPH: Our windows didn't get soaped.

STEWART: Our pumpkin didn't get smashed.

STEPH: It was like they didn't want to offend us with their demonic visages.

STEWART: Not that there *were* any demonic— *(Aside to STEPH.)* Demonic what?

STEPH: I may be an English teacher, but I also know some French.

STEWART: I wanted vampires, space monsters—serial killers. I wanted prostitutes, porn stars—stabbing victims. I watched. I waited. But walking by were only kids dressed like superheroes and homeless people.

STEPH: Bums.

STEWART: Bums take no effort.

STEPH: I wanted effort.

STEWART: I wanted somebody to really try.

STEPH: Remembrance Day?

STEWART: Nobody remembered.

STEPH: And as there was no Legion—

STEWART: Nobody drank. Even at the school, the principal—

STEPH: He wanted to work it into his Remembrance Day "all-call", but he didn't know how.

STEWART: Instead, he stuck with the standard "moment of silence".

STEPH: One minute—sixty seconds of silence.

STEWART: In which I started to talk. *(Jumping out of his chair.)* I asked "Who watched the game last night?" I said, "For lunch there's sesame chicken." I said, "It's cold—it's really cold."

STEPH: It was November.

STEWART: It was supposed to be cold.

STEPH: It was cold so everything was okay.

STEWART: Everything was right.

STEPH: Everything was fine.

Brief pause.

STEWART: But Christmas. *(Sitting down.)* It's a special time, Christmas.

STEPH: With the trees, the snow.

STEWART: The Santas. The specials on TV.

STEPH: It was my turn.

STEWART: It was—for a realization.

STEPH: My turn—my realization.

STEWART: It was more a continuation.

STEPH: A what?

STEWART: An add-on. A further add-on to mine.

STEPH: Everybody died.

STEWART: You'd say that, right?

STEPH: Everybody's dead.

STEWART: You'd say it's a further add-on to mine?

STEPH: Our family, friends—and not only friends, plain ol'

acquaintances had missed Thanksgiving, Halloween, Remembrance Day and now Christmas. And, okay, maybe Remembrance Day isn't a "gather your family around the fire" kinda day, but it had been missed. And it would be missed. It'd be missed next year, the next year and the next next year after that.

STEWART: Steph?

STEPH: We're alone—him and me. Me and him. Him and—

STEWART: Steph.

STEPH: No.

STEWART: Your eyes.

STEPH stands.

STEPH: *(Forcefully.)* I said "no". We need friends—new friends. Other people. Any people.

STEWART: Which is funny, 'cause—

STEPH: Which is hilarious, 'cause—

STEWART: That's about when Trish knocked.

STEPH turns to face front. STEWART moves in behind her.

STEPH: She said, "Merry Christmas! Did you get our card?"

STEWART: Then she asked if we had eaten her lasagna, her chili—her meatloaf and her squares.

STEPH: Her chocolate squares with bits of coconut.

STEWART: See, Trish was asking for her casserole dishes, the microwave-safe Tupperware, and her glass-bottom pans.

STEPH: But not if we were using them.

STEWART: If we were, she could improvise.

STEPH: If we weren't, she needed them back.

STEWART: She was having a party.

STEPH: She planned to be entertaining.

STEWART: That's it— "entertaining" —that's what she was gonna be.

STEPH: "Oh", I said.

STEWART: "A party", I said.

STEPH: "What kind of party?" I asked.

STEWART: "And who are you inviting?"

Beat.

STEPH: There was a pause.

STEWART: Her mouth—it sort of hung.

STEPH: Her mouth—it kinda fell.

STEWART: And then her mouth—her mouth started moving.

STEPH: "New Year's," she said.

STEWART: "You know—December thirty-first?"

STEPH: "And did you—?"

STEWART: "You" being Steph— "you" being me.

STEPH: "Would you like to come?"

Brief pause. STEWART and STEPH turn together to move to the corner of the stage. Unidentifiable music strikes up from overhead.

STEWART: Trish had a nice house.

STEPH: A century house.

STEWART: We talked about the process of restoration.

STEPH: "The process of restoration." Trish talked.

STEWART: Trish lectured.

STEPH: And we—we feigned interest.

STEWART: Her sons—her twin male sons got stuck serving drinks.

STEPH: At school I'm their teacher.

STEWART: She's their teacher—I'm their librarian.

STEPH: It's not the same.

STEWART: It's a position of authority.

STEPH: It's not the same when you're drinking in front of students. You shouldn't drink in front of students.

STEWART: You shouldn't, but you did.

STEPH: I got nervous.

STEWART: You threw up outside.

STEPH: You got nervous.

STEWART: But I didn't throw up outside.

STEPH: It was the guests.

STEWART: Trish's guests. Trish's "eclectic menagerie".

STEPH: There was people we didn't know.

STEWART: Were.

STEPH: People we'd seen—but didn't know.

STEWART: And there we were.

STEPH: There we sat.

STEWART: Talking.

Brief pause.

We talked about sports teams.

STEPH: Mr. Trish was *very* big on football.

Brief pause.

STEWART: We talked about the food.

STEPH: There was a spinach dip, a Mexican dip and a cheese fondue.

Brief pause.

STEWART: We talked about the weather.

STEPH: How it was cold, really cold—but surprisingly not much snow.

Brief pause.

STEWART: We talked about movies.

STEPH: Serious movies—not the kind with J-Lo.

STEWART: And.

STEPH: There's an "and".

STEWART: And then at midnight we counted.

STEPH: Ten.

STEWART wanders away from STEPH towards centre-stage.

STEWART: We played a game.

STEPH: Nine.

STEWART: "Pick a memory".

STEPH: Eight.

STEWART: The best memory of the year.

STEPH: Seven.

STEWART: Now make a wish.

STEPH: Six.

STEWART: Some kinda wish for the future.

STEPH: Five.

STEWART: But don't say your wish for the future.

STEPH: Four.

STEWART: Never say your wish for the future.

STEPH: Three.

STEWART: It won't come true.

STEPH: Two.

STEWART: I wished for a future.

STEPH: One.

STEWART: Some kind—any kind of future.

STEPH: *(Without enthusiasm.)* Happy New Year.

STEWART: And I didn't say. I wanted to say—I was tempted, but instead I said, "Does anybody need anything? I mean, anything? I'm talking lamps; I'm talking fishing rods. I'm taking patio furniture, coffee makers, lawn mowers and beds. I'm talking picture frames, shower curtains and floor-to-ceiling bookcases. I'm talking towel holders, tool kits and hair-shaping accessories. You don't have to say now. This might not be the time. But let me know. Gimme a call. 'Cause Steph and I—we've inherited fourteen houses—

STEPH walks across to join STEWART.

STEPH: Fifteen.

STEWART: *(To STEPH.)* Fourteen. At that point the fifteenth had yet to clear.

STEPH: Fourteen.

STEWART: Fourteen homes—each one full of stuff we hadn't even gone through yet.

STEPH: Not that we didn't want to.

STEWART: We just—we didn't want to.

STEPH: And Trish?

STEWART: The ever-positive, always-thinking, "Trish"?

STEPH: "Trish" short for "Trish-a"?

STEWART: But don't call her that. Don't ever call her that. She said—

STEPH: "Sell it."

STEWART: Like that.

STEPH: She talked about spiritual beginnings.

STEWART: She talked about symbolic rebirths.

STEPH: She talked a lot—she even offered to help.

STEWART: She said to have a yard sale—but not a "yard" sale 'cause all your stuff, there's not really a "yard" that'll fit it. Call up the principal, take him out, buy him a few drinks and then buy him some more. Ask to use the football field for one weekend—one day. Have a "football field" sale and sell it off. Sell everything. "Sell it." Like that.

STEPH: She even offered to help.

STEWART: She did.

STEPH: She wanted to help. And Stewart and me—

STEWART: Stewart and I—

STEPH: *(With great frustration.)* Stewart and I—

STEWART: We did what Trish suggested.

STEPH: I was a good idea—a good plan.

STEWART sits casually.

STEWART: We talked to the principal.

STEPH: I talked to the principal.

STEWART: The principal—he doesn't like me.

STEPH: He likes you. He just thinks you're useless.

STEWART: *(To the audience.)* He doesn't like me.

STEPH: He thinks having a librarian is useless.

STEPH sits.

STEWART: Dead weight on the payroll.

STEPH: See? He likes you fine. He said, "yes" to our proposal.

STEWART: He didn't say, "yes" —he said, "we'll see".

STEPH: He had some worries.

STEWART: Holes in the field.

STEPH: Traffic on the lawn.

STEWART: What would we do with what we wouldn't sell?

STEPH: I said we'd take care of it.

STEWART: I'm not useless.

STEPH: I said we had help. I told him we had Trish. The principal—he knew Trish. And because he knew Trish, he knew everything would be fine.

Brief pause.

STEWART: Steph?

STEPH: What?

STEWART: You okay?

STEPH: Yeah.

STEWART: You good?

STEPH: We're there.

STEWART: Almost.

STEPH: We're almost there.

Brief pause.

STEWART: We started two weeks after New Year's.

STEPH: We thought, "Why wait?" "Why take our time?"

STEWART: "Why waste the help when we need it"? And suddenly—

STEPH: Instantly—

STEWART: Surprisingly—time wasn't measured in holidays.

STEPH: Valentine's Day? He didn't send roses.

STEWART: I saved the sixty bucks.

STEPH: Or chocolate—

STEWART: Twenty bucks.

STEPH: He didn't even give me a card.

STEWART: Cards are a needless expense.

STEPH: For dinner we had cereal and ice cream.

STEWART: Instead of going out, we stayed in.

STEPH: Instead of sex we went to bed.

STEWART: For March Break we'd planned on Florida.

STEPH: Orlando, Florida.

STEWART: Trish suggested Disneyland.

STEPH: We bought tickets, but we didn't go.

STEWART: I'd never been.

STEPH: It's Florida.

STEWART: Instead of holidays our weeks got split into houses, rooms, basements, attics—doors that hadn't been opened in months.

STEPH: And Trish.

STEWART: Poor Trish. Stepping into that first house.

STEPH: Breathing in that stale air.

STEWART: Trish started to cry.

STEPH: And hearing the silence of that house—

STEWART: Trish really started to cry.

STEPH: See, back on New Year's—?

STEWART: Her shoulders, they started shaking.

STEPH: Exactly what she was getting into, Trish had no idea.

STEWART: We sat Trish down.

STEPH: Stewart - he taught her some tricks.

STEWART: I said, "Close your eyes, Trish".

STEPH: She didn't get this—not at first.

STEWART: Trish was worried it was all a little "sexual".

STEPH looks across to STEWART.

STEPH: It wasn't sexual.

STEWART: Nothing's sexual—not with Trish. I said, "Close your eyes and think of the door in front of you, the handle all cold and steel. Think of the carpet you're standing on and the shade of green it used to be. Think of the textured wallpaper but don't think—never think "God, that's ugly" or "What was Grandpa thinking?" but above all above everything never think "I remember that from when I was four."

Brief pause.

STEPH: The next few months we packed stuff.

STEWART: We priced stuff.

STEPH: Some stuff we even kept.

STEWART: I kept shoes. Leather shoes. I kept the kind of shoes that you'd only wear on Sunday. And not just men's shoes—I kept women's shoes, too. I'll never wear the women's shoes—I'll probably never wear the men's shoes, either—but I wanted to be consistent. I wanted to be fair. I kept shoes.

STEPH: I kept crap.

STEWART: She kept crap.

STEPH: I kept useless crap. Gadgets. Keepsakes. Souvenirs. Crap. And that might seem pointless—that might seem kinda weird, but things like mini-statues of the Tower of London and party hats saved from the millennium meant something to somebody not too long ago. It's in our basement—

STEWART: Next to my shoes.

STEPH: A great big box of crap.

Brief pause.

STEWART: One night, Trish—

STEPH: This was probably two—three months into the year.

STEWART: One night Trish—she asked a favour.

STEPH: She asked for a moment—a minute of our time.

STEWART: She'd invited a friend—

STEPH: Not "friend" —she didn't say that.

STEWART: She'd invited a guest. An important guest. She'd invited the Mayor.

STEPH: Glencoe's Mayor.

STEWART: And some veterans—she'd invited them, too. They wanted to talk about the Legion. Or at least, what used to be the Legion. They wanted to talk about the Legion that used to be there.

STEPH: Now we'd inherited some money.

STEWART: A little money. Okay, a lot of money.

STEPH: We didn't know how much. We'd never counted.

STEWART: Not that we didn't want to.

STEPH: We just—we didn't want to.

STEWART: But the Mayor—

STEPH: Glencoe's Mayor.

STEWART: We didn't vote for him.

STEPH: We didn't vote against him, either.

STEWART: He was asking for a donation.

STEPH: "It wasn't your fault what happened."

STEWART: He wanted to say that—he wanted us to know.

STEPH: Even so.

STEWART: Even so we said we'll have to wait.

STEPH: We said we'll have to see.

STEWART: We said, "We're waiting for the yard sale."

STEPH: But not a "yard" sale.

STEWART: "The football field" sale—we're waiting to see what we sell on the day.

STEPH: Trish apologized after.

STEWART: She was mortified by the situation.

STEPH: Trish regretted asking us for the moment—for the minute of our time.

STEWART: See, Trish was well intentioned.

STEPH: Trish—she only wanted to help.

Brief pause. STEWART stands, moving downstage.

STEWART: The day was perfect. No rain.

STEPH: Nothing. Trish offered to drive us.

STEWART: In her Honda. She was waiting.

STEPH: She was parked outside. But not Mr. Trish—

STEWART: He camped all night at the school with the boys.

STEPH: Her twin male sons. They were security.

STEWART: Trish wanted security.

STEPH: She didn't want anything stolen, missing, or standing up and walking away.

STEWART: That morning, Main Street—

STEPH: We're not just talking road.

STEWART: Sidewalks. Stores. Even lights in houses.

STEPH: No sign of anything.

STEWART: No sign of life.

STEPH: But the street coming up to the high school—

STEWART: Both sides, both ways.

STEPH: Full.

STEWART: Packed.

STEPH: And we'd said, "no early birds".

STEWART: We'd said "nothing before nine", but people—

STEPH: All the people.

STEWART: And the cars—but not really cars. More like station wagons—pickup trucks. Cube vans rented special for the occasion.

STEPH: Trish thought we shouldn't be there.

STEWART: She thought we should be elsewhere.

STEPH: "Take in a movie" —no, not "movie", "take in a *matinee.*"

STEWART: Get dressed up. Go for dinner. She was concerned.

STEPH: She wanted us out of there.

STEWART: She was worried.

STEPH: She wanted us out of there.

STEWART: She was sensitive.

STEPH: She wanted us out of there.

STEWART: And that's when I noticed.

STEPH: That's when we saw.

STEWART: A little pile.

STEPH: More like a stack.

STEWART: My grandmother's couch and some paintings by my Aunt Joan. A "Laz-E-Boy" from one of Steph's cousins and a garden hose that was my Grandpa Roy's. A flower vase that used to be my mother's—a tie rack that was my dad's. There were some clothes that used to be my sister's and other things—other things I couldn't recognize or tried not to place. There were other things. Other things in the pile.

STEPH stands, joining STEWART downstage.

STEPH: I asked Mr. Trish politely.

STEWART: You did. You were very nice.

STEPH: I asked Mr. Trish what the hell that stuff—what it was doing there.

STEWART: But in a nice way. She was very nice.

STEPH: Mr. Trish said it was "a few things".

STEWART: "A few things his wife had stashed away." And Steph—

STEPH: And I.

STEWART: And you, Steph—

STEPH: And I—

STEPH stares straight ahead throughout STEWART's speech, not registering any emotion.

STEWART: I saw her. I watched Steph as she walked across the track and through the soccer posts heading for Trish. I didn't stop her. I could have—I could have said, "Close your eyes and think of cheesecloth" but I didn't. I didn't say anything. But Steph—Steph said months of things. Steph said holidays and rooms and breakfasts and TV shows and trashy novels of things. She said—

Brief pause.

She.

Brief pause.

She—

STEPH stares blankly ahead. Without emotion—

STEPH: Eleven months ago we left our wedding—we got changed in the basement of the Glencoe Branch of the Royal Canadian Legion, we climbed into our car and left. And our family, our friends—our acquaintances we were considerate enough to invite stayed behind. And somewhere between songs, between pictures, between beers being handed over the bar—the gas that had been leaking *oh so slowly* in the kitchen blew. The air became orange with fire and the emergency lights over the doorways that were supposed to never went on. Sons tried to rescue their mothers, grandparents tried to rescue each other and wives tried to rescue their men. And in the midst of all that rescuing—in the midst of all that clawing for hope nobody made it out of our wedding alive.

Brief pause.

STEWART: Trish was hearing her. Trish was listening to what she was saying. But what Trish was seeing—? What everybody on that football field was seeing was death. Was Steph—was me covered in death. And that's when I realized—that's when I knew that death is what we are now. That's what Steph is—and me, that's me.

STEPH looks across to STEWART.

STEPH: And looking back at Stewart—?

STEWART looks across to STEPH.

STEWART: Looking out at Steph I knew—

STEPH: We knew.

STEWART: I will be with you forever.

Brief pause.

STEWART: We quit the school a few days later.

STEPH: We packed our things and moved away.

STEWART and STEPH stand together, charming and casual.

STEWART: And now—?

STEPH: Right now—?

STEWART: We need new friends.

STEPH: We need new people.

STEWART: New acquaintances, new chums.

STEPH: And this story—all of this story.

STEWART: It's just a story.

STEPH: Think of it that way.

STEWART: Remember it that way.

STEPH: We could say, "please."

STEWART: It was something to say.

Brief pause.

STEPH: We're gonna go now.

STEWART: We hafta leave.

STEPH: It's not that we wanna—we'd love to stick around.

STEWART: Have a drink.

STEPH: Maybe four.

STEWART: Talk awhile—maybe about you. But we can't.

STEPH: We can't. Not tonight.

STEWART starts to pull STEPH away.

STEWART: This is the part where you congratulate us.

STEPH: This is the part where you wave.

STEWART: This is where you wish us "Happy Anniversary".

STEPH: And this is the part where we go.

STEWART walks off, with STEPH slighty behind. STEPH looks back at the audience, awkward and uncomfortable. She address them—

STEPH: Don't worry.

STEWART: It wouldn't happen.

STEPH: Not again.

STEWART: We're gonna go.

STEPH: It's all right.

STEWART: Steph? We hafta go.

STEPH: We'll see you soon.

STEWART: *(To the audience.)* Just close your eyes.

STEPH: Think about something.

STEWART: Close your eyes.

STEPH: Think about anything.

STEWART: Close your eyes.

STEWART & STEPH: Now.

Blackout.

The End.